ENGLISH AT WORK

Book One
Finding a Job

H. R. Arnold, M. J. Fitzgerald, I. D. Maclachlan

HULTON EDUCATIONAL

First published in Great Britain 1982
by Hulton Educational Publications Ltd
Raans Road, Amersham, Bucks HP6 6JJ

Text © Hilary R. Arnold, Michael J. Fitzgerald
and Ian D. Maclachlan 1982
Illustrations © Hulton Educational Publications Ltd 1982

ISBN 0 7175 0989 3

Printed in Great Britain by
The Pitman Press, Lower Bristol Road, Bath

ACKNOWLEDGEMENTS
With thanks to our colleagues and students at the
Industrial Language Centre, Slough College of Higher
Education and also to Barney Aldridge, who drew the
illustrations. H.R.A. M.J.F. I.D.M.

Contents

Introduction

Finding a Job, with its related cassette, is the first part of a two-part course called *English at Work*. It has been written mainly for students whose first language is not English but who want to work in factories, shops or other businesses where English is used. For this reason it concentrates on practising the sort of everyday English needed to find your way round a town or place of work. It also develops the skills you need when looking and applying for a job.

Each Unit deals with different aspects of looking for a job, and is divided into two Sections. These Sections are made up of illustrations or charts, and exercises based on them. Your teacher will guide you through these exercises and the symbols at the beginning of each one will give you an idea of the sorts of answer expected.

Finding a Job will help you to do exactly that — find a job. It cannot guarantee that you get the job once you have applied for it, but it will help you to put yourself across in a way likely to give you the best possible chance.

Further material in the *English at Work* course:
Book Two   ISBN 0 7175 1012 3
Teacher's Book   ISBN 0 7175 1017 4

Cassette: Book One   ISBN 0 7175 1013 1
Cassette: Book Two   ISBN 0 7175 1014 X

UNIT 1

FINDING THE WAY

In this unit you will learn how to find your way around a town or factory. You will ask for, receive and then give directions, as well as read both a town and factory plan.

Section A
Focus: The Town Plan

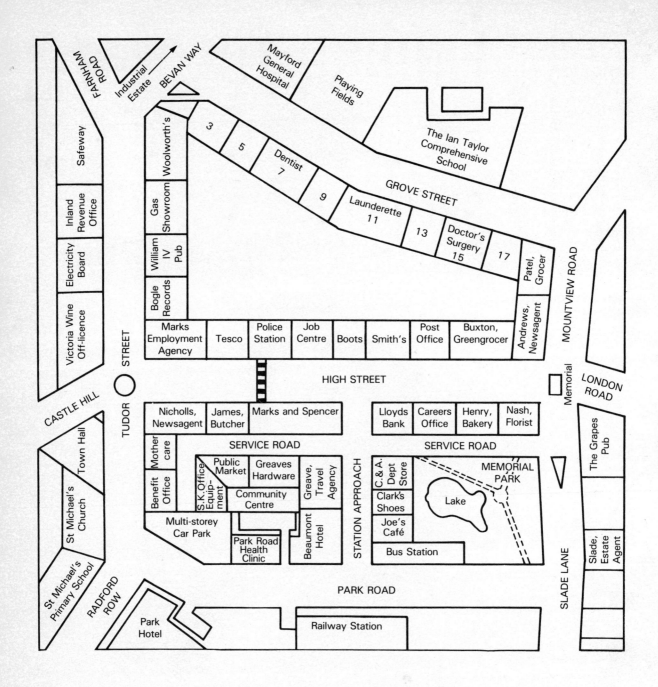

FARNHAM ROAD

Industrial Estate

BEVAN WAY

Safeway

Inland Revenue Office

Electricity Board

Victoria Wine Off-licence

CASTLE HILL

TUDOR STREET

St Michael's Church

Town Hall

St Michael's Primary School

RADFORD ROW

Woolworth's

Gas Showroom

William IV Pub

Bogle Records

Mayford General Hospital

Playing Fields

3

5

Dentist 7

9

Launderette 11

13

The Ian Taylor Comprehensive School

GROVE STREET

Doctor's Surgery 15

17

Patel, Grocer

Andrews, Newsagent

MOUNTVIEW ROAD

Marks Employment Agency

Tesco

Police Station

Job Centre

Boots

Smith's

Post Office

Buxton, Greengrocer

HIGH STREET

Memorial

LONDON ROAD

Nicholls, Newsagent

James, Butcher

Marks and Spencer

Lloyds Bank

Careers Office

Henry, Bakery

Nash, Florist

SERVICE ROAD

SERVICE ROAD

Mothercare

Benefit Office

Public Market

S.K. Office Equipment

Greaves Hardware

Greave, Travel Agency

Community Centre

Multi-storey Car Park

Park Road Health Clinic

Beaumont Hotel

STATION APPROACH

C. & A. Dept Store

Clark's Shoes

Joe's Café

Bus Station

MEMORIAL PARK

Lake

The Grapes Pub

Slade, Estate Agent

SLADE LANE

PARK ROAD

Park Hotel

Railway Station

Exercise 1: Using the Town Plan — Boxend

A

Look at the street plan of Boxend and, with a partner, answer the following questions. (Use *in* in your replies.)

Example: Your partner: 'Excuse me, where is the Job Centre?'
        You: '*In* the High Street.'
  i. 'Excuse me, where is the Police Station?'
 ii. 'Excuse me, where is the Careers Office?'
iii. 'Excuse me, where is the Bus Station?'
iv. 'Excuse me, where is the Benefit Office?'

Now ask your partner where the following places are:
   v. The Employment Agency
  vi. The Town Hall
 vii. The Inland Revenue Office
viii. The Ian Taylor Comprehensive School
  ix. The Post Office

B

Look at the street plan again and answer these questions. (Use *next to* in your replies.)

Example: Your partner: 'Excuse me, where is Tesco's?'
        You: '*Next to* the Police Station.'
  i. 'Excuse me, where is Buxton's?'
 ii. 'Excuse me, where is Smith's?'
iii. 'Excuse me, where is Woolworth's?'
iv. 'Excuse me, where is Safeway's?'

Now ask your partner where the following places are:
   v. Joe's Café
  vi. Clark's Shoes
 vii. St Michael's Primary School
viii. The Beaumont Hotel
  ix. Henry's Bakery

C

Look at the street plan again and answer the following questions.
(Use *between* in your replies.)

Example: Your partner: 'Excuse me, where is the butcher's?'
   You: '*Between* Marks and Spencer's and the Newsagent's.
  i. 'Excuse me, where is Tesco's?'
 ii. 'Excuse me, where is the Post Office?'
iii. 'Excuse me, where is Clark's Shoe Shop?'
 iv. 'Excuse me, where is St Michael's Church?'

Now ask your partner where the following places are:
   v. The Doctor's Surgery
  vi. The Launderette
 vii. The Health Clinic
viii. The Dentist's
  ix. The Police Station

D

Look at the street plan again and answer the following questions.
(Use *on the corner of* in your replies.)

Example: Your partner: 'Excuse me, where is the Town Hall?'
   You: '*On the corner* of Castle Hill and Tudor Street.'
  i. 'Excuse me, where is the Grapes Pub?'
 ii. 'Excuse me, where is Patel's?'
iii. 'Excuse me, where is Marks Employment Agency?'
 iv. 'Excuse me, where is the Park Hotel?'

Now ask your partner where the following places are:
   v. The Victoria Off-Licence
  vi. Woolworth's
 vii. Nash's
viii. The Newsagent's
  ix. The Multi-storey Car Park

E Find the Place

Complete the following with the name of a shop or other building:
  i. This is between Tesco's and the Job Centre.
     It is ....
 ii. This is between Boots and the Post Office.
     It is ....
iii. This is between Joe's Café and C. & A.'s Department Store.
     It is ....
 iv. This is next to the Town Hall.
     It is ....
  v. This is next to Nash's.
     It is ....
 vi. This is next to the Health Clinic.
     It is ....
vii. This is opposite Tesco's.
     It is ....
viii. This is opposite Greave's Travel Agency.
     It is ....
 ix. This is opposite the Post Office.
     It is ....
  x. This is on the corner of Mountview Road and Grove Street.
     It is ....

F True or False?

Check these sentences. Write (T) for True or (F) for False after each one.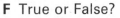

  i. The Bus Station is in Slade Lane.   (   )
 ii. The Job Centre is in the High Street   (   )
iii. The Town Hall is on the corner of Tudor Street
     and Radford Row.   (   )
 iv. Boots is between Smith's and the Post Office.   (   )
  v. Lloyds Bank is next to the Careers Office.   (   )
 vi. Marks Employment Agency is on the corner of the
     High Street and Tudor Street.   (   )
vii. The Police Station is next to the Job Centre.   (   )
viii. The Benefit Office is in the High Street.   (   )
 ix. The Inland Revenue Office is in Tudor Street.   (   )
  x. The Careers Office is opposite the Post Office.   (   )

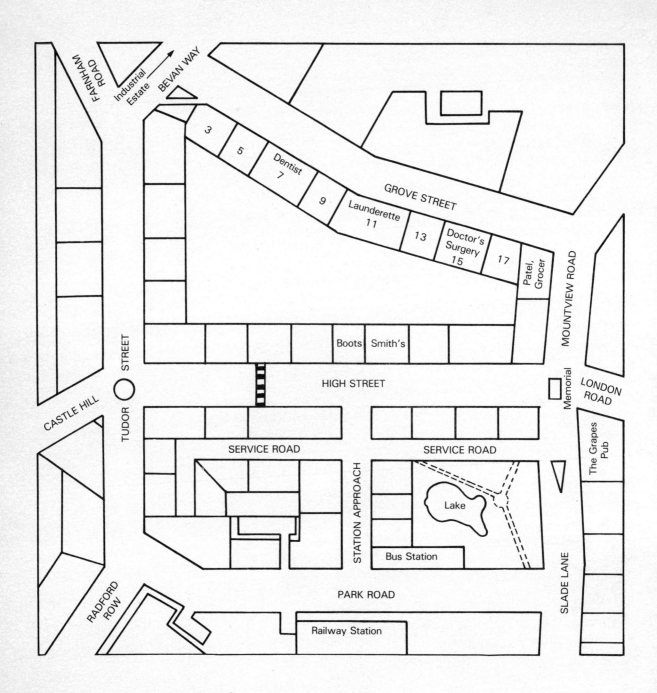

FARNHAM ROAD

Industrial Estate

BEVAN WAY

3
5
Dentist 7
9
Launderette 11
13
Doctor's Surgery 15
17
Patel, Grocer

GROVE STREET

MOUNTVIEW ROAD

TUDOR STREET

CASTLE HILL

Boots Smith's

HIGH STREET

Memorial

LONDON ROAD

SERVICE ROAD

SERVICE ROAD

The Grapes Pub

STATION APPROACH

Lake

Bus Station

SLADE LANE

RADFORD ROW

PARK ROAD

Railway Station

10

Exercise 2: Following Directions

Look at the street plan opposite. Follow the taped directions with
your finger and find the places.

A

You are standing outside Boots. I'm going to tell you how to get to:
 i. *The Gas Showroom.*   Go along the High Street to Tudor
   Street. Turn right and the Gas Showroom is the fourth shop on
   the right. Point to the Gas Showroom.
 ii. *Andrews the Newsagent's.*   Go down the High Street to
   Mountview Road. Andrews the Newsagent's is on the corner of
   the High Street and Mountview Road. Point to Andrews the
   Newsagent's.
 iii. *St Michael's Church.* Go along the High Street to Tudor Street.
   Turn left and St Michael's Church is the second on the right.
   Point to St Michael's Church.

B

You are standing outside the Bus Station. I'm going to tell you how
to get to:
 i. *The Travel Agency.*   Turn right along Park Road, then right
   again down Station Approach. Greave's Travel Agency is the
   second on the left. Point to the Travel Agency.
 ii. *The Town Hall.*   Turn right along Park Road, bear right and
   the Town Hall is on the corner of Tudor Street and Castle Hill.
   Point to the Town Hall.
 iii. *The Estate Agent's.*   Turn left along Park Road. Go past the
   Memorial Park and turn left into Slade Lane and cross it. The
   Estate Agent's is the second on your right, next-door-but-one to
   the Grapes Pub. Point to the Estate Agent's.

Exercise 3: Giving Directions

Look at the first street plan on page 6. With a partner, complete the
following dialogues.

A

You are standing outside Tesco's.
Example: x: Excuse me. Can you tell me the way to Lloyds Bank?
          y: Yes. Go straight along the High Street and it's on your
             right.
          x: Thanks.
 i.   x: Excuse me. Can you tell me the way to Henry's
             Bakery?
          y: ....
          x: Thanks.

Example: x: Excuse me. Can you tell me the way to the Post Office?

y: Yes. Go straight along the High Street and it's on your left.

x: Thanks.

ii.   x: Excuse me. Can you tell me the way to the Job Centre?

y: ....

x: Thanks.

Remember you are outside Tesco's. Now tell your partner the way to:

iii. The Careers Office   v. Smith's
iv. Marks and Spencer's   vi. The Greengrocer's

B

You are standing outside Lloyds Bank. Complete the following dialogues with a partner.

Example: x: Excuse me. Could you tell me where the Benefit Office is?

y: Yes. Go along the High Street, turn left into Tudor Street and it's on your left.

x: Along the High Street and turn left into Tudor Street?

y: Yes.

x: Thank you.

i.   x: Excuse me. Could you tell me where Patel's is?

y: ....

x: Along the High Street and turn left into Mountview Road?

y: ....

x: Thank you.

Example: x: Excuse me. Could you tell me where the Gas Showroom is?

y: Yes. Go straight along the High Street, turn right into Tudor Street and it's on the right.

x: Straight along the High Street and turn right into Tudor Street?

y: Yes.

x: Thank you.

ii.   x: Excuse me. Could you tell me where Woolworth's is?

y: ....

x: Straight along the High Street and turn right into Tudor Street?

y: ....

x: Thank you.

Now tell your partner how to find these places:

iii. Mothercare   v. St Michael's Church
iv. Bogle's Records   vi. Electricity Board

UNIT 1

Section B
Focus: The Factory Plan

Site Plan of Turner, Islip and Son Limited

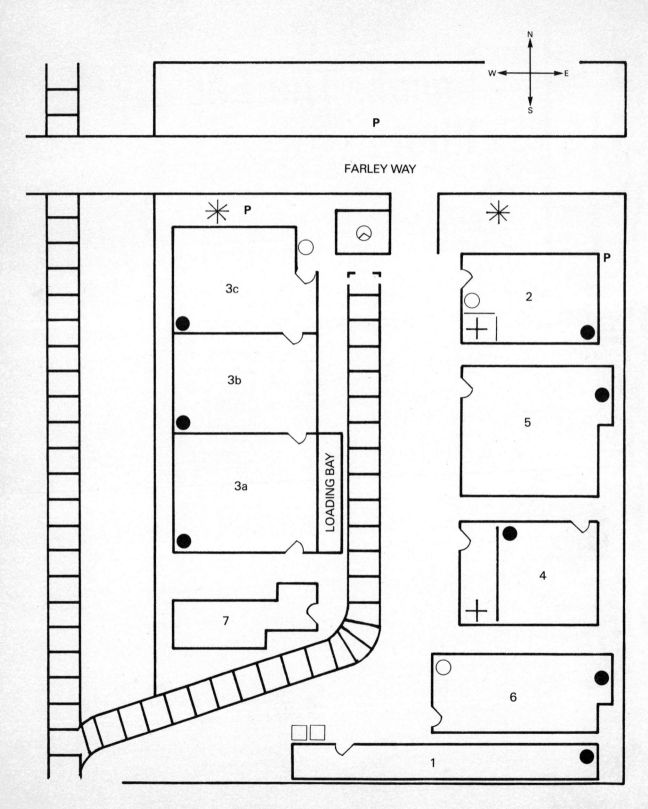

FARLEY WAY

Exercise 1

Using the information on the plan, complete the following exercises:

A Getting to Know the Symbols

Match these phrases with the symbol in the key below

Example: A place to leave your car: ....**P**

  i. A place to go for petrol ....

 ii. A place to go after an accident ....

iii. A place to change your clothes ....

 iv. A place to go if there is a fire ....

  v. A place to read notices ....

SYMBOL	KEY
⊗	Clock Station Office
●	Toilets/Locker Rooms
○	Notice Boards
+	First Aid Points
✳	Fire Assembly Points
P	Car Parks
☐	Petrol Pump
∧	Doors

B Getting to Know the Numbers

Look at the key below and complete the following exercise:

	Number	*Place*
Example: A place where typists work	2	The Main Office
i. You eat here	....	....
ii. You get new supplies here	....	....
iii. Things are made here	....	....
iv. Lorry drivers report here	....	....
v. Things are repaired here	....	....

NUMBERS	KEY
1	Garage
2	The Main Office
3a	Production Line A
3b	Production Line B
3c	Production Line C
4	Canteen
5	Maintenance
6	Stores
7	Transport Department

C Checking the Symbols

Using the site plan, answer the following questions:

Example: How many Fire Assembly Points
are there? ....Two...

  i. How many First Aid Stations are
there? ....
  ii. How many Toilets and Locker Rooms
are there? ....
  iii. How many Car Parks are there? ....
  iv. How many Notice Boards are
there? ....
  v. How many Petrol Pumps are
there? ....

D True or False?

Check these sentences. Write (T) for True
and (F) for False after each one.
  i. The Maintenance Store is between the
First Aid Points. ( )
  ii. The Car Parks are on the north side of
the site. ( )
  iii. The Petrol Pumps are on the south side
of the site. ( )
  iv. Production Line B is between
Production Line A and
Transport. ( )
  v. The Clock Station is opposite the
Maintenance Store. ( )

E Giving Directions

Look at the site plan and, with a partner,
answer the following questions:
Example: How do you get from Production
Line B to Transport?
Go through Production Line A,
out of the door, cross the Yard
and Transport is on the right.
  i. How do you get from Production Line
C to the Canteen?

  ii. How do you get from the Garage to the
Clock Station?
  iii. How do you get from Production Line
A to the nearest First Aid Point?
  iv. How do you get from the Clock Station
Car Park to the Store?
  v. How do you get from the Canteen to
the Main Office?

F Where are you?

Look at the site plan and follow the taped
directions.
Example: You are in the Main Office.
Go out of the Main Office, cross
the Yard and it's on your right.
Where are you?
At the Clock Station.

  i. You are in the canteen.
Go out of the door, turn left, cross the
Yard and it's opposite you.
Where are you?
....
  ii. You are in the Transport Department.
Go out of the door. Turn right, go
straight ahead and it's in front of you.
Where are you?
....
  iii. You are in Production Line A.
Go out of the south door, turn left,
cross the Yard and it's in front of you.
Where are you?
....
  iv. You are in Production Line B.
Go through Production Line C, turn
right. Cross the Yard and it's the first
building on your right.
Where are you?
....
  v. You are in the Clock Station Car Park.
Go past the Clock Station, cross the
Yard and go along to the fourth
building on your left.
Where are you?
....

UNIT 2

TIME AND TIMETABLES

In this unit you will look at different ways of telling the time, using both a 12-hour and a 24-hour clock. In Section B you will look at bus and train timetables, and also study a few daily work schedules.

Section A
Focus: Clocks

Exercise 1: Telling the Time

A On the Hour

i. Say these times:

ii. Put these times on the clocks:

1.00   **4.00**   **6.00**   **10.00**

 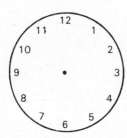  

B Past the Hour

i. Say these times:

18

ii. Put these times on the clocks:

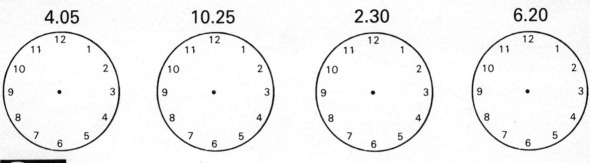

4.05   10.25   2.30   6.20

C To the Hour

i. Say these times:

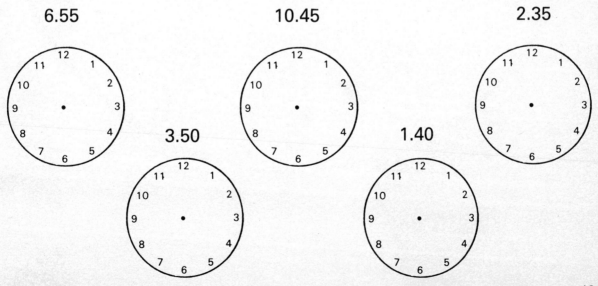

ii. Put these times on the clocks:

6.55   10.45   2.35

3.50   1.40

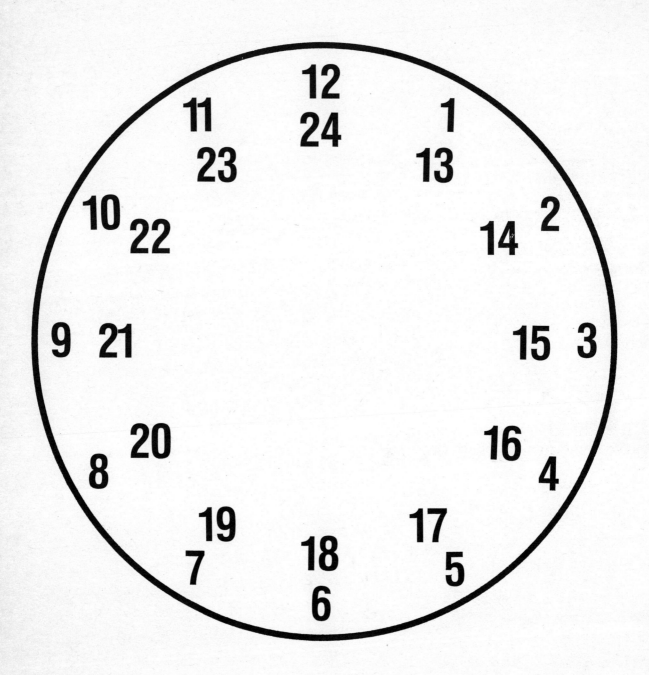

Exercise 2: Telling the Time — the 24-hour Clock

A Before Noon
Look at the 24-hour clock. Now look at these examples:

1 a.m. = 01.00
1 p.m. = 13.00

and do the same for the times written below:
   i.   = 06.00
  ii. 3 a.m. =
 iii. 8 a.m. =
 iv.   = 07.00
   v. 9 a.m. =
 vi. 11 a.m. =
 vii.   = 10.00
viii.   = 04.00
 ix. 2 a.m. =
  x. 12 noon =

B After Noon
Look at these examples:

12 noon = 12.00
 1 p.m. = 13.00
 2 p.m. = 14.00

Now use the 24-hour clock and do the same for the times written below:
   i. 3 p.m.   =
  ii. 10 p.m.   =
 iii.   = 16.00
 iv.   = 18.00
   v. 5 p.m.   =
 vi.   = 21.00
 vii.   = 23.00
viii. 12 midnight =
 ix. 7 p.m.   =
  x.   = 20.00

C

Draw the following times on to the clock faces:

13.00	16.00	20.00
22.00	04.00	17.00
18.00	21.00	15.00
08.00	14.00	03.00

UNIT 2

Section B
Focus:
Timetables and Charts

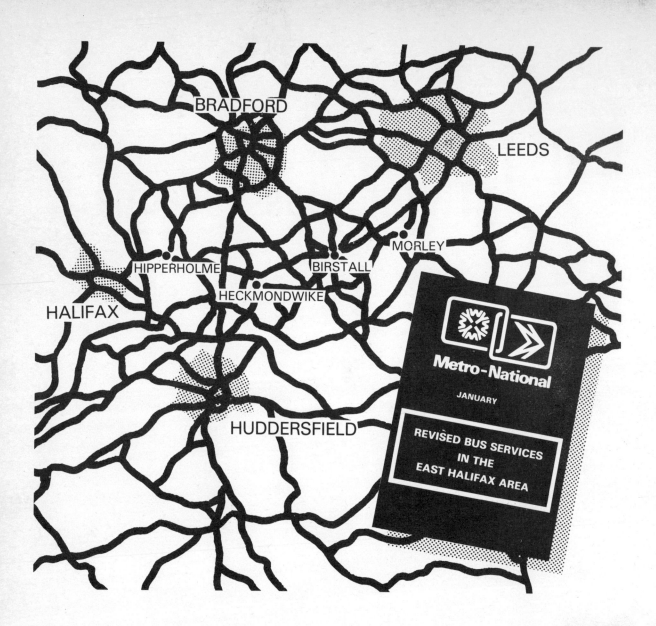

Leeds - Halifax via Morley, Heckmondwike and Cleckheaton   ≫ *Service* **226**

Monday to Saturday

Pay As You Enter

Leeds Sovereign Street ≅				0710		10		1710	1810	1910	2010	2110		2210
Old Lane			■	0721		21		1721	1821	1921	2021	2121		2221
Morley Town Hall			0633	0733		33		1733	1833	1933	2033	2133		2233
Bruntcliffe Angel Inn			0639	0739	Then at	39		1739	1839	1939	2039	2139		2239
Howden Clough			0643	0743	these	43		1743	1843	1943	2043	2143		2243
Birstall Market Place			0646	0746	minutes	46	until	1746	1846	1946	2046	2146		2246
Heckmondwike Green	0557	0617	0657	0757	past each	57		1757	1857	1955	2055	2155		2257
Cleckheaton Bus Station	0607	0627	0707	0807	hour	07		1807	1907					2307
Pack Horse Inn	0612	0632	0712	0812		12		1812						
Bailiff Bridge	0618	0638	0718	0818		18		1818						
Hipperholme Cross Roads	0624	0644	0724	0824		24		1824						
Halifax Bus Station	0634	0654	0734	0834		34		1834						

Exercise 1: Bus and Train Timetables

A Getting About by Bus
Look at the bus timetable on the opposite page and answer the following questions:

You are at Leeds Sovereign Street bus stop, next to the Railway Station:

  i. It is 11.30 on a Wednesday.
    When is the next bus to Cleckheaton Bus Station? ....

  ii. It is 09.25 on a Thursday.
    When is the next bus to Morley Town Hall? ....

  iii. It is 23.00 on a Friday.
    When is the next bus to Halifax Bus Station? ....

You are at Leeds Old Lane bus stop:
  iv. It is 18.00 on a Thursday.
    When is the next bus to Heckmondwike Green? ....

  v. It is 15.15 on a Monday.
    When is the next bus to Hipperholme Cross Roads? ....

B True or False?
Look at the timetable again and say whether the following statements are True (T) or False (F):

  i. The bus service runs from Cleckheaton Bus Station
    to Morley Town Hall.   (   )
  ii. The 226 is a weekday service.   (   )
  iii. The 07.10 bus from Leeds Sovereign Street arrives
    at the Pack Horse Inn at 08.07.   (   )
  iv. The bus service number is 206.   (   )
  v. The bus calls at Bailiff Bridge.   (   )
  vi. The last bus from Cleckheaton Bus Station is at
    18.07.   (   )
  vii. Buses leave Leeds Sovereign Street every two
    hours between 07.10 and 17.10.   (   )
  viii. The 3.33 p.m. bus from Morley Town Hall stops at
    all bus stops.   (   )
  ix. The last through bus to Halifax leaves Leeds Old
    Lane at twenty-one minutes past five.   (   )
  x. There are no buses on Saturdays.   (   )

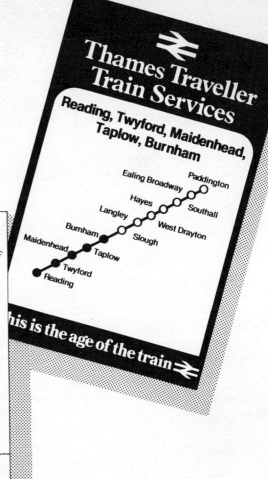

Thames Traveller Train Services

Reading, Twyford, Maidenhead, Taplow, Burnham

Ealing Broadway · Paddington · Hayes · Southall · Langley · West Drayton · Burnham · Slough · Maidenhead · Taplow · Twyford · Reading

This is the age of the train

Reading→Maidenhead→Slough→London
Mondays to Fridays For fast service READING→LONDON→PADDINGTON see page 15 **Local services only**

← departures (Reading–Burnham) → | ← arrivals (Slough–Paddington) →

Reading	Twyford	Maidenhead	Taplow	Burnham	Slough	Langley	West Drayton	Hayes & Harlington	Southall	Ealing Broadway	Paddington
		00 08x	→	→	00 15x					00 33xs	00 45x
04 35	→	04 48	→	→	04 56	05 14	05 22	05 26	05 30	05 39	05 52
05 57	06 04	06 13	06 17	06 20	06 27	06 34	06 42	06 46	06 50	06 44	06 54
06 27	06 34	06 43	06 47	06 50	06 57	07 14	07 05			07 15	07 25
06 52	06 59	07 08	07 12	07 15	07 22	07 36	07 44	07 48	07 52	07 36	07 46
07 12	07 20		→	→	07 37	07 56	08 04	08 08	08 12	08 04	07 59
		07 33	07 37	07 40	07 47	07 56	08 04	08 08	08 12	08 04	08 14
		07 43	→	→							08 11
07 34	07 42	07 53	07 57	08 01	08 07	08 16	08 24	08 28	08 32	08 25	08 36
07 45	→	→	→	→	08 04	08 16	08 24	08 28	08 32	08 39	08 25
		07 53	→	→							08 28
07 50	07 57	08 06	08 10	→	08 17	08 34	08 42	08 46	08 50	08 44	08 39
		08 13	08 17	08 20	08 27	08 34	08 42	08 46	08 50	08 44	08 54
08 15	08 22	08 30	→	→							08 59
		08 33	08 37	08 40	08 47	08 54	09 02	09 06	09 10	09 04	09 16
08 37	08 44	08 53	08 57	09 00	09 07	09 14	09 22	09 26	09 30	09 24	09 36
08 47	08 54	09 03	→	→	09 07	09 14	09 22	09 26	09 30	09 24	09 27
		09 13	09 17	09 20	09 27	09 34	09 42	09 46	09 50	09 44	09 56
09 22	09 29	09 38	09 42	09 45	09 52	10 04	10 12	10 16	10 20	10 09	10 19
	09 39	09 48	→	→	→	→	→	→	→	10 12	10 22
09 52	09 59	10 08	10 12	10 15	10 22	10 34	10 42	10 46	10 50	10 39	10 49
10 22	10 29	10 38	10 42	10 45	10 52	11 04	11 12	11 16	11 20	11 09	11 19
10 43	→	→	→	→	10 57					→	11 16
10 52	10 59	11 08	11 12	11 15	11 22	11 34	11 42	11 46	11 50	11 39	11 49
11 22	11 29	11 38	11 42	11 45	11 52	12 04	12 12	12 16	12 20	12 09	12 19
11 43	→	→	→	→	11 57					→	12 16
11 52	11 59	12 08	12 12	12 15	12 22	12 34	12 42	12 46	12 50	12 39	12 49
12 22	12 29	12 38	12 42	12 45	12 52	13 04	13 12	13 16	13 20	13 09	13 19
12 45	→	→	→	→	12 59					→	13 18
12 52	12 59	13 08	13 12	13 15	13 22	13 34	13 42	13 46	13 50	13 39	13 49
13 22	13 29	13 38	13 42	13 45	13 52	14 04	14 12	14 16	14 20	14 09	14 19
13 52	13 59	14 08	14 12	14 15	14 22	14 34	14 42	14 46	14 50	14 39	14 49
13 53	→	→	→	→	14 07					14 39	14 26
14 22	14 29	14 38	14 42	14 45	14 52	15 04	15 12	15 16	15 20	15 09	15 19
14 43	→	→	→	→	14 57					→	15 16
14 52	14 59	15 08	15 12	15 15	15 22	15 34	15 42	15 46	15 50	15 39	15 49
15 22	15 29	15 38	15 42	15 45	15 52	16 04	16 12	16 16	16 20	16 09	16 19
15 45	→	→	→	→	15 59					→	16 18
15 52	15 59	16 08	16 12	16 15	16 22	16 34	16 42	16 32	16 36	16 43	16 53
16 17	16 24	16 33	16 37	16 40	16 47	16 54	17 02	16 57	17 01	17 08	17 18
16 37	16 44	16 53	16 57	17 00	17 07	17 15	17 23	17 17	17 21	17 28	17 38
16 43	→	→	→	→	16 57	17 15	17 23	17 17	17 21		17 16
16 58	→	→	→	→	→	→	→	→	→	17 23s	17 35
16 57	17 04	17 13	17 17	17 20	17 27	17 34	17 42	17 37	17 41	17 48	17 58

Heavy figures indicate through train; light figures indicate a change of train is necessary

x – Mondays excepted   s – calls to set down only   continued→

C Getting About by Train

Look at the train timetable on the opposite page and answer the questions below:

You are in Slough station on Wednesday.

   i. It is 12.05. When is the next train to London?

   ....

   ii. It is 11.35. When is the next train to London?

   ....

   iii. It is 10.45. When is the next train to London?

   ....

   iv. It is 09.55. When is the next train to London?

   ....

   v. It is 08.40. When is the next train to London?

   ....

   vi. It is 05.55. When is the next fast train to London?

   ....

   vii. It is 13.15. When is the next fast train to London?

   ....

   viii. It is 14.05. When is the next train to Langley?

   ....

   ix. It is 15.00. When is the next train arriving in Slough?

   ....

   x. It is 17.20. When is the next train arriving in Slough?

   ....

   xi. It is 16.25. When is the next train arriving in Slough?

   ....

   xii. It is 05.22. When is the next train to Ealing Broadway?

   ....

   xiii. It is 10.28. When is the next fast train arriving in Slough?

   ....

   xiv. How many trains stop at Slough between 11.00 and 12.00?

   ....

   xv. How many trains stop at Slough between 10.00 and 11.00?

   ....

   xvi. I want to arrive in London before 11.30. What train should I catch?

   ....

   xvii. I want to arrive in Langley before 10.25. What train should I catch?

   xviii. I want to arrive in Langley at 11.04. What train should I catch?

   ....

27

Exercise 2: Daily Timetables

A

John Davis is unemployed. He is looking for work. This is his daily timetable. Describe his day and then complete your daily timetable.

Your Daily Timetable

TIME	JOHN DAVIS
7.30	get up
7.45	eat breakfast
8.30	catch bus to town
9.00	visit Job Centre
10.00	sign on at Benefit Office
11.00	go round Industrial Estate
1.00	have lunch
2.00	walk home
5.00	have tea
6.00	watch T.V.

TIME	
	get up
	have lunch

B Routine at Work

Look at the work schedules opposite. Now complete the chart.

	HARBANS KAUR	IRIS MURRAY	JACK JONES
Time allowed for tea/coffee breaks:			
Time allowed for lunch:			
Time allowed for clocking on:			
Time spent working:			
Total break time:			
Total time at workplace:			

WORK SCHEDULES

HARBANS KAUR
7.55 clock on
8.00 start work
10.00 break for tea
10.15 start work
12.00 lunch break
12.30 start work
2.45 tea break
3.00 start work
4.00 clock off

IRIS MURRAY
9.00 start work
10.30 coffee break
10.50 start work
1.00 lunch break
2.00 start work
3.00 tea break
3.20 start work
4.45 stop work

JACK JONES
7.20 clock on
7.30 start work
9.45 tea break
10.00 start work
12.00 lunch break
12.45 start work
2.45 tea break
3.00 start work
4.15 clock off

C Comparing Work Routines
Now answer the following questions:

i. Who has the longest day? ....

ii. Who has the most working time? ....

iii. Who has the most break time? ....

iv. Who has the shortest lunch time? ....

v. Who has the shortest working time? ....

D Travelling to and from work

Read the following text and, using the timetable below, complete the chart with the times of the buses used.

Harry Evans lives at Lye Cross and has a job in a supermarket in Stourbridge. He starts work at 8.30 a.m. and finishes at 6.00 p.m. Bill Jones lives at Brierley Hill and works for a light engineering company in Dudley. He works a system of rotating shifts: in the first week he does 8.00 a.m. to 2.00 p.m., in the second week he does 2.30 p.m. to 10.00 p.m. and in the last week 10.30 p.m. to 6.30 a.m.

STOURBRIDGE - DUDLEY   via Pedmore Fields   Service 294

Monday to Saturday

STOURBRIDGE, Bus Station ⇌	0627	0702		1732	1802	1832	1932	2032	2132	2232
Junction Station ⇌	0631	0706		1736	1806	1836	1936	2036	2136	2236
Pedmore Fields, Queensway	0635	0710	then	1740	1810	1840	1940	2040	2140	2240
Hodge Hill, Worton Road	0637	0712	every	1742	1812	1842	1942	2042	2142	2242
Wynall Estate, Traffic Island	0641	0716	30 mins	1746	1816	1846	1946	2046	2146	2246
Lye Cross, Pedmore Road ⇌	0647	0722	until	1752	1822	1852	1952	2052	2152	2252
Brierley Hill, Danilo	0658	0733		1803	....	1903	2003	2103	2203	2303
DUDLEY, Bus Station	0713	0748		1818	....	1918	2018	2118	2218	....

DUDLEY, Bus Station	0717	0752		1822		2222	....
Brierley Hill, Midland Bank	0732	0807		1837		2237	2307
Lye Cross, Pedmore Road ⇌	0743	0818	then	1848	then	2248	2318
Wynall Estate, Traffic Island	0749	0824	every	1854	hourly	2254	2324
Hodge Hill, Worton Road	0753	0828	30 mins	1858	until	2258	2328
Pedmore Fields, Queensway	0755	0830	until	1900		2300	2330
Junction Station ⇌	0759	0834		1904		2304	2334
STOURBRIDGE, Bus Station ⇌	0803	0838		1908		2308	2338

CODE: ⇌—Near Rail Station.

	HARRY EVANS	BILL JONES
WEEK 1 Bus to work: Bus home:		
WEEK 2 Bus to work: Bus home:		
WEEK 3 Bus to work: Bus home:		

UNIT 3

JOBS AND PEOPLE

In this unit you will find out about the jobs different people do. You will also learn where these people work in a factory.

Section A
Focus: Job Charts

Exercise 1

A Filling in a Job Chart

Look at the first line of the job chart below. When you listen to the tape you will hear that Ali Mohammed unloads lorries, so in his column a tick has been placed against 'Labourer'.

Now listen to the tape and complete the chart in the same way for all three workers.

	ALI MOHAMMED	MARY JONES	SHANTA KUMARI
Labourer	√		
Receptionist			
Packer			
Factory			
Office			
Overalls			
Coat			
14 days			
21 days			
24 days			
Clean job			
Dirty job			

B Using Information from a Table

	FRED SLADE	RAM SINGH	LILY MORGAN
Job	Supervisor	Machine operator	Canteen assistant
Place	Factory	Factory	Canteen
Clothes	White coat	Overalls	Green coat
Holidays	27 days	21 days	14 days

C Using Information from a Table

	JASWANT SINGH	GURDIP KAUR	TESSA SKUZA	MARIA BLANCO
Packer				X
Laundry attendant			X	
Canteen assistant		X		
Loader	X			
26 days' holiday				X
21 days' holiday		X	X	
24 days' holiday	X			
Works: 8.00–5.00			X	X
Works: 8.00–5.30	X			
Works: 9.00–3.00		X		

Using the information above, take it in turns with a partner to describe Fred Slade, Ram Singh and Lily Morgan.

Complete the following sentences, using the information above:
Example: Maria Blanco is a *packer*.......
    She has *26 days' holiday* a year........
    She works from *8.00–5.00* five days a week

i. Jaswant Singh is a ....
   He has .... a year.
   He works from .... five days a week.
ii. Gurdip Kaur is a ....
   She has .... a year.
   She works from .... five days a week.
iii. Tessa Skuza is a ....
   She has .... a year.
   She works from .... five days a week.

33

D
Describe the following people, using all the information given below:
Example: Kuldip Kaur is a packer. She works in a . . .
  i. Kuldip Kaur – packer – factory – overalls – 20 days
 ii. Sohan Singh – loader – warehouse – blue overalls – 21 days
iii. Jack Wilson – personnel manager – office – suit – 28 days

E True or False?
Put a tick in the appropriate box: T (True) or F (False)

                                                                    T   F

  i. Clive Baines is a labourer.
    a. He works in an office.
    b. He drives a fork lift truck.
    c. He does heavy work.
    d. He doesn't wear overalls.
 ii. Mrs Chagger is an inspector in the packing department.
    a. She works in a factory.
    b. She drives a van.
    c. She checks quality.
    d. She doesn't tell people what to do.
iii. Mohammed Sidique is a bus driver.
    a. He works in a factory.
    b. He works on his own.
    c. He works shifts.
    d. He doesn't wear a uniform.

F Yes or No?
Answer 'yes' or 'no' to the following questions:

  i. Ali is a labourer. He sweeps and cleans the factory.
    a. Does he work with his hands? ....
    b. Does he work indoors? ....
    c. Does he make things? ....
    d. Does he drive a lorry? ....
    e. Does he wear a uniform? ....
    f. Does he work with people? ....
 ii. Aisha is a supervisor in a biscuit factory.
    a. Does she work out of doors? ....
    b. Does she give orders? ....
    c. Does she work with people? ....
    d. Does she have responsibility? ....
    e. Does she wear a uniform? ....
    f. Does she work with machines? ....

UNIT 3

Section B
Focus: A Site Plan

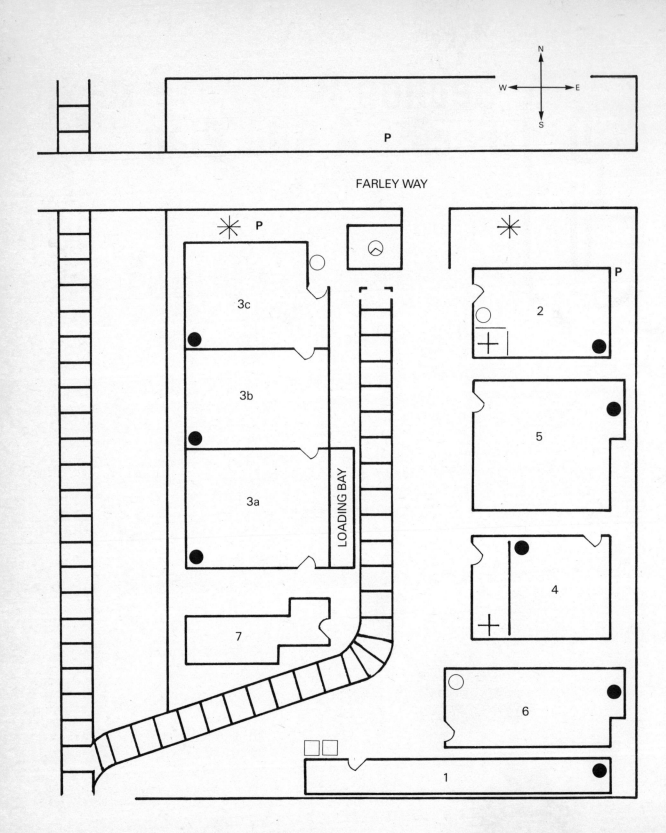

FARLEY WAY

LOADING BAY

Exercise 1

A Looking at a Factory

Look at the site plan of Turner, Islip and Son Ltd. Listen to what the Personnel Manager says on the tape and find the words that mean the same as:

i. Put together
ii. Cardboard boxes
iii. Put
iv. Loading platform
v.

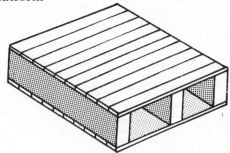

vi.

vii. A branch railway line
viii.

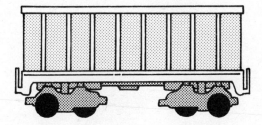

ix. Repair
x. Gives out

B Describing a Factory

Choose the right word from this list and complete the following description of Turner, Islip and Son Ltd:

Main Office	next	west
Production Departments	between	south
Petrol Pumps	near	site
Production Line C	opposite	store

Turner, Islip and Son Ltd is a small company. It has three _____ _____ These are on the _____ side of the _____ That is where all the products are made. Line C is _____ Farley Way. Line A is _____ to the Transport Department.

The Main Office is _____ the Clock Station. It is a small building on the left as you enter the site. Maintenance is _____ the Main Office and the Canteen. Broken machines are repaired there.

The Garage is on the _____ side of the factory. Lorries are serviced there. The _____ _____ are in front of the Garage. There are three Notice Boards, one in the _____, one in the _____ and one in _____ _____ _____.

C Where do these People Work?

Example: Fred / Engineer
You: What does Fred do?
Your partner: He's an engineer. He works in maintenance.

  i. Mary Smith / Packer   iv. Gurdev Singh / Mechanic
  ii. Carol Jones / Receptionist   v. Bill Collins / Security Officer
 iii. Naseem Akhtar / Typist

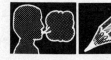

D Where do these People Work?

Example: Anna is a secretary. She works in the office.

  i. Mike is a loader.   He works _____
  ii. Tom is a storeman.   He works _____
 iii. Mary is a cook.   She works _____
 iv. George is a cutter.   He works _____
  v. Kuldip is an engineer.   He works _____

E Describing the Jobs.

Complete the following:

Turner, Islip and Son _____ metal boxes. They _____ three Production Lines. On Production Line A they _____ metal boxes. On the next Line they _____ the boxes and on Line C they _____ the boxes into cartons. On the Loading Bay labourers _____ the cartons onto lorries. Engineers _____ machines when they stop working. The storeman _____ materials to the supervisors. In the Main Office the receptionist _____ visitors.

UNIT 4

JOBS AND PLACES

In this unit you will learn more about factory
jobs and places of work. You will also be asked to
think about the kind of job you would like to do.

Section A
Focus:
Plan of a Workplace

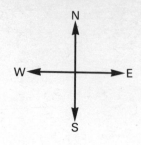

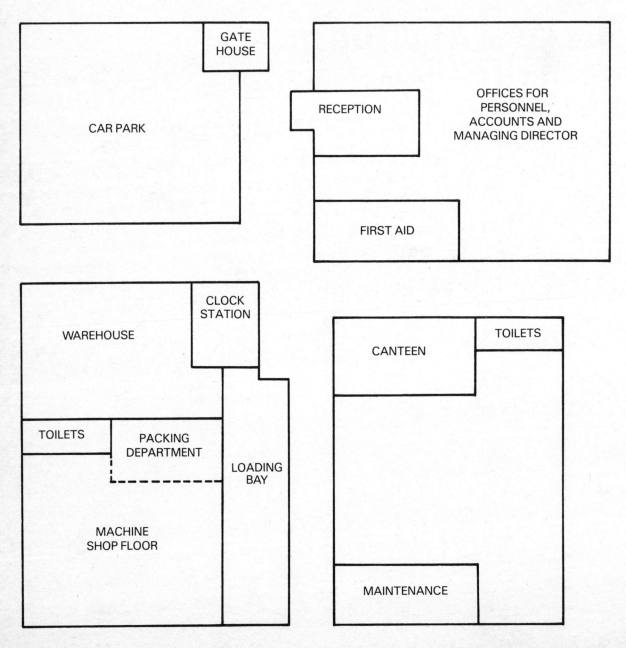

GATE HOUSE

CAR PARK

RECEPTION

OFFICES FOR PERSONNEL, ACCOUNTS AND MANAGING DIRECTOR

FIRST AID

WAREHOUSE

CLOCK STATION

TOILETS

PACKING DEPARTMENT

LOADING BAY

MACHINE SHOP FLOOR

CANTEEN

TOILETS

MAINTENANCE

Exercise 1: At Work

A People at Work

Look at the drawings below of some of the people who work in a factory. Label each person with his or her job, using the words in the box to help you.

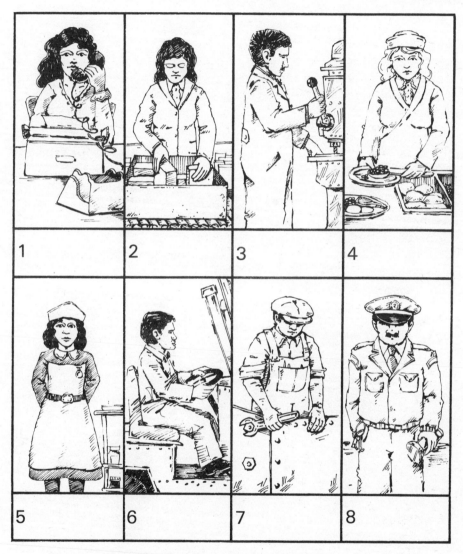

Canteen Assistant	Fork-lift Driver
Fitter	Packer
Nurse	Machine Operator
Security Officer	Receptionist

B Places of Work

Look at the plan of the factory. Read the passage below and match the jobs with the factory work areas.

Example: Clock Station   *Security Officer/Gateman*

In a factory a canteen assistant works in the canteen. A labourer and a fork-lift driver may work in a loading bay or in a warehouse. A packer works in the packing department, a fitter works in maintenance and a nurse works in first aid. A security officer and gateman will usually work near the clock station. A wages clerk, a personnel manager, an accountant, a production manager and a secretary have offices. A chargehand, a foreman, a supervisor, a machine operator and an assembler work on the shop floor while a receptionist works in reception.

Jobs in a factory

Canteen assistant	Works manager
Labourer	Production manager
Packer	Machine operator
Assembler	Receptionist
Engineer/Fitter	Secretary
Chargehand/Foreman	Personnel manager
Wages clerk	Nurse/First aider
Supervisor	Fork-lift driver
Security officer/Gateman	

Factory work areas

Clock Station   ....

First Aid   ....

Loading Bay   ....

Packing   ....

Office   ....

Warehouse/
Storage   ....

Canteen   ....

Maintenance   ....

Reception   ....

Shop Floor   ....

C Who Works Where?

Write in the answers to the following questions:

Example: Question: Who works in the canteen?

            Answer: A canteen assistant.

  i. Who works in the loading bay?

....

 ii. Who works in the warehouse?

....

iii. Who works in the packing department?

....

 iv. Who works on the machine shop floor?

....

  v. Who works in reception?

....

 vi. Who works in the first aid room?

....

vii. Who works in the workshop?

....

viii. Who works in the personnel department?

....

 ix. Who works on the gate?

....

  x. Who works in the accounts office?

....

D Who's This?

Write in the names of the jobs which fit the following descriptions:

Example: She works in the canteen. She serves food and clears the
           dirty dishes. She wears green overalls.

           Answer: A canteen assistant.

  i. He wears a uniform. He meets people coming to the factory and
gives them directions. He checks the factory at night. He works
on the gate.

    Answer: ....

 ii. He wears overalls. He's a skilled man. He repairs machinery. He
keeps his tools in the maintenance department.

    Answer: ....

iii. He wears blue overalls. He works in most departments. He uses
a broom. He clears away the rubbish.

    Answer: ....

 iv. She doesn't wear a uniform. She answers all telephone calls to the
factory. She receives visitors. She works in the entrance to the
office block.

    Answer: ....

  v. He works on the machine shop floor. He makes things on the
machine. He reports to a supervisor. He wears overalls.

    Answer: ....

E Filling in the Plan

Using the information below, complete the blank factory plan.

1 (Example) The main entrance is at the north end of the site.
2 The gate house is on the west of the main entrance.
  There is a car park behind the gate house.
3 Next to the car park is the stores department.
4 The clock station is in the corner on the east side of the stores department.
5 The packing department is between the stores and the production department.
6 The loading bay is on the east side of the production department.
7 Across the yard from the loading bay is the maintenance department.
8 Opposite the stores is a large office block.
9 Reception is in the middle of the west side of the office block.
10 The first aid station is in the south west corner of the maintenance block.
11 The canteen and social club are at the south end of the site.
12 There is a second car park south of the social club.

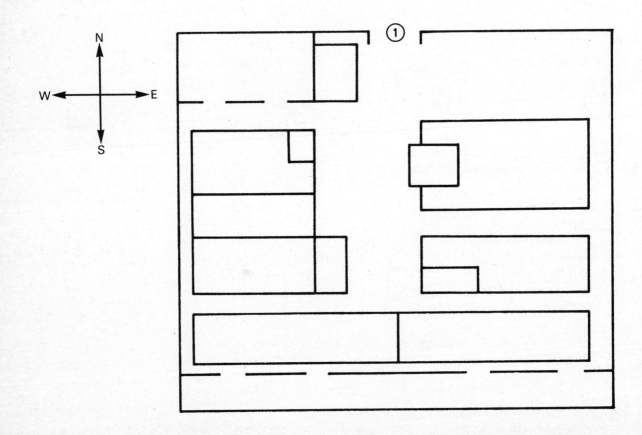

UNIT 4

Section B
Focus: Questionnaires

Exercise 1: Types of Job

A Yes or No?

Answer these questions by putting a tick in the appropriate box:

	Yes	No
i. Is a cleaner a skilled worker?	☐	☐
ii. Is a fitter a skilled worker?	☐	☐
iii. Is a typist a skilled worker?	☐	☐
iv. Is a postman a skilled worker?	☐	☐
v. Is a canteen assistant a semi-skilled worker?	☐	☐
vi. Is a telephonist a semi-skilled worker?	☐	☐
vii. Is a labourer a semi-skilled worker?	☐	☐
viii. Is a machine operator a semi-skilled worker?	☐	☐
ix. Is a packer a semi-skilled worker?	☐	☐
x. Is a bus driver an unskilled worker?	☐	☐
xi. Is a plumber an unskilled worker?	☐	☐
xii. Is a carpenter an unskilled worker?	☐	☐
xiii. Is a doctor a professional worker?	☐	☐
xiv. Is a milkman a professional worker?	☐	☐
xv. Is a teacher a professional worker?	☐	☐

B Workers

Complete the following statements, using one of these phrases:

A professional worker   A semi-skilled worker
An unskilled worker   A skilled worker

i. .... follows a special training course and learns a particular skill.

ii. .... studies for a number of years after secondary school and gets a qualification.

iii. .... starts work without any special training or qualification.

iv. .... gets some training at his place of work.

C Look at the following jobs.

Write them in the appropriate columns of the table below.

Labourer	Engineer	Plasterer
Nurse	Canteen assistant	Inspector
Packer	Chef	Milkman
Chemist	Dentist	Shop assistant
Machine setter	Bus conductor	Cleaner

SKILLED	UNSKILLED	PROFESSIONAL

Exercise 2

A Choosing the right job

Answer the following questions by putting a tick in the appropriate box.

	Yes	Don't know	No
Example: Do you like working with your hands?	☐	☐	☐
i. Do you like working out of doors?	☐	☐	☐
ii. Do you like working indoors?	☐	☐	☐
iii. Do you like doing clean work?	☐	☐	☐
iv. Do you like working with machines?	☐	☐	☐
v. Do you like driving?	☐	☐	☐
vi. Do you like making things?	☐	☐	☐
vii. Do you like assembling things?	☐	☐	☐
viii. Do you like typing?	☐	☐	☐

	Yes	Don't know	No
ix. Do you like wearing a uniform?	☐	☐	☐
x. Do you like taking orders?	☐	☐	☐
xi. Do you like meeting people?	☐	☐	☐
xii. Do you like serving people?	☐	☐	☐
xiii. Do you like working with people?	☐	☐	☐
xiv. Do you like working with animals?	☐	☐	☐
xv. Do you like working on your own?	☐	☐	☐

B

But are you prepared to do the following?

	Yes	No
i. Are you prepared to work shifts?	☐	☐
ii. Are you prepared to wear a hair-net?	☐	☐
iii. Are you prepared to cut your beard?	☐	☐
iv. Are you prepared to work in a shop?	☐	☐
v. Are you prepared to work in an office?	☐	☐
vi. Are you prepared to work in a factory?	☐	☐
vii. Are you prepared to travel to work?	☐	☐
viii. Are you prepared to work overtime?	☐	☐
ix. Are you prepared to work public holidays?	☐	☐
x. Are you prepared to take responsibility?	☐	☐
xi. Are you prepared to obey workplace regulations?	☐	☐
xii. Are you prepared to have training?	☐	☐

UNIT 5

LOOKING AT ADVERTISEMENTS

In Section A you will look at advertisements and learn to work out exactly what they are saying. Section B takes a closer look at the requirements for different jobs.

Section A
Focus: Advertisements at the Job Centre

Exercise 1: At the Job Centre

A Job Centre Vacancy Cards

At the Job Centre vacancies are advertised on cards like this:

JOBCENTRE

(MAN OR WOMAN)

JOB
DISTRICT
BUSINESS
PAY
HOURS
DETAILS
ASK FOR JOB No.

Match the following words with words from the card:

Vacancy ....   Area ....

Male ....   Female ....

Wages ....   Time worked ....

Comments ....   Type of work ....

Reference Number ....

B

JOB	Receptionist/Typist	(MAN OR
DISTRICT	Trading Estate	WOMAN)
BUSINESS	Light engineering	
PAY	Negotiable	
HOURS	9.00 a.m. – 5.00 p.m. Monday to Friday (with one hour lunch break)	
DETAILS	Answer telephone Copy and audio typing Deliver post and wages	
ASK FOR JOB No.	3803	

Look at the advertisement above and answer the following questions:

i. What is the job? ....

ii. Where is it? ....

iii. How much money will you get? ....

iv. How many hours a week? ....

v. What do you have to do? ....

vi. What is the reference number? ....

C True or False?

Write 'True' or 'False' in answer to the following statements:

i. The vacancy is for a telephonist. ....

ii. The job is in the town centre. ....

iii. The wages are fixed. ....

iv. The working week is 35 hours. ....

v. You have to meet visitors. ....

vi. You have to answer the phone. ....

vii. You need to be a typist ....

viii. Experience is necessary. ....

ix. You must deliver the post. ....

x. There is overtime on Saturdays ....

D Job Centre Abbreviations

Look at the advertisement below, then match the following words with abbreviations from the card.

		(MAN OR WOMAN)
JOB	Accts.clerk	20/25 pref.
DISTRICT	T. Est.	
BUSINESS	Upholsterers	
PAY	Neg.	
HOURS	37½	
DETAILS	2 yrs. accts exp. pref. 'O' level maths. Wk. in a small team. Every aspect of accts. and admin.	
ASK FOR JOB No.	361	

Accounts .... *Accts.*   Trading Estate ....

Administration ....   Years ....

Experience ....   Work ....

Negotiable ....   Preferred ....

E

Look at the list of jobs below. Place each one under one of the three headings provided in the table.

JOBS IN OFFICES	JOBS IN FACTORIES	MISCELLANEOUS
Secretary	Labourer	Bus driver

Secretary	Fireman	Night watchman	Fork-lift truck driver
Labourer	Welder	Policeman	Security guard
Bus driver	Cashier	Plumber	Assembler
Packer	Sales assistant	Capstan operator	Fitter
Receptionist	Painter	Wages clerk	Press operator
Printer	Carpenter	Telephonist	Cook
Postman	Telex operator	Machine operator	Clerk

 F

JOBCENTRE

(MAN OR WOMAN)

Machine operator / labourer 20's – 30's
Trading estate
£1.60 per hr. to start
8.00 – 4.30 Monday to Friday
Operate various machines to make tin boxes, etc.
May also deliver and collect goods in Co. van.
Must have clean driving licence.
Machine operator's exp. not essential.

32961

Look at the above Job Centre Vacancy Card and complete the form as far as possible.

DETAILS FROM JOB CENTRE VACANCY CARD	
i. Job	....
ii. Hourly rate of pay	....
iii. Hours	....
iv. Experience needed	....
v. Special conditions	....
vi. Preferred age of applicant	....
vii. location of job	....

UNIT 5

Section B
Focus: Newspaper Advertisements

54

Exercise 1: Newspaper Advertisements

A

Look at the advertisements on the opposite page. Match them with the jobs listed below:

Example: Ad. 1   – Postman/Postwoman

.................................– Machinist

.................................– Driver

.................................– Assembly worker

.................................– Fitter

.................................– Roofing labourer

.................................– Clerk/Typist

.................................– Storeman

.................................– Office worker

B Conditions of Work

Match the ads with the work conditions listed below:

Example: Ad. 3   – Life insurance provided free

.................................– Social club

.................................– Help with bus fares

.................................– Long annual holidays

.................................– Staff shop

.................................– Pension scheme fund

.................................– Canteen

C Details of the Job

Select one of the jobs in the adverts and complete the form below:

THE COMPANY ....

THE JOB ....

WHAT SORT OF JOB? (Put a tick in the appropriate boxes)

☐   Indoors

☐   Out-of-doors

☐   Skilled

☐   Unskilled

☐   Semi-skilled

☐   Heavy

☐   With a lot of people

☐   Alone

☐   Well-paid

☐   Clerical

☐   Dirty

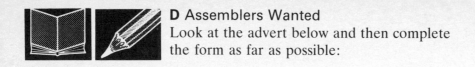

D Assemblers Wanted
Look at the advert below and then complete
the form as far as possible:

CRISPIN & SONS LTD.
105, Banbury Avenue
Urgently Required

ASSEMBLERS

To work rotating shifts in our new factory.
Shift allowance, subsidised Canteen,
Pension Scheme & Social Club.
Overtime may be available.

Telephone:
Mrs. Smithers
Personnel Manager
No: 55431 ext. 76

CRISPIN AND SONS LIMITED
i. Name of the company
ii. Address
iii. Job
iv. How do you apply?
v. Who do you apply to?
vi. Allowances
vii. Overtime
viii. Fringe benefits

E
Fill in similar forms for two adverts chosen from your local paper.

F Comparing Jobs
Two factory jobs are described below:

SMITH'S CHOCOLATE FACTORY	MAIN ROAD PLASTICS
Overtime – a quarter of wage	Overtime – none
Piecework – no	Piecework – yes
Canteen – full cost	Overalls – not provided by management
Overalls provided	Transport provided
No travelling	Subsidised canteen
New clean building	Old and dirty building

Now answer the following questions:

i. Which job allows overtime? ....

ii. Which job has pleasant work conditions? ....

iii. Which job has below cost meals? ....

iv. Which job is local? ....

v. Which job provides protection
for your clothes? ....

vi. Which job would you choose? ....

G What the Job Offers

Look at the adverts below.

GOLLAN & SON

Labourers wanted for
weekend working.
Transport provided.
Top rates
Dirty work bonus.
Travel time paid.
Phone 69978 Ext. 79
Ask for Mr. Johnson

SAFE SERVICE LTD.
- Security guard required
  - 3-shift system
  - Shift bonus
  - Weekend bonus
- References required
  - Must be fit
- Driving licence essential

- Phone Reg Vale on 45312

WISLOWS & CO.

PACKERS
Part-time evening work
Good rates for
piecework

Phone 36519 or call at
Security

HARBOYS & GIDDY LTD.
Fitter wanted
Overtime available

Apply in writing to
Box No. 361

Now say whether the following statements are true or false by
writing T (True) or F (False) in the appropriate boxes:

  i. Safe Service Ltd. do not require references. ☐
 ii. Safe Service Ltd. work a two-shift system. ☐
iii. There is no overtime at Safe Service Ltd. ☐
 iv. The security guard must be in good health. ☐
  v. The guard does not need to drive. ☐
 vi. The workers at Safe Service earn bonuses. ☐
vii. A fitter is needed at Harboys & Giddy. ☐
viii. The fitter must be able to drive a lorry. ☐
 ix. The fitter can work overtime if he wishes. ☐
  x. The fitter must phone for the job. ☐
 xi. Mr. Johnson works for Safe Service Ltd. ☐
xii. Gollan & Son provide transport. ☐
xiii. Gollan & Son pay badly. ☐
xiv. Workers for Gollan & Son do not work at weekends. ☐
 xv. Gollan & Son offer clean work. ☐
xvi. Wislows do not have a phone. ☐
xvii. Wislows need full-time workers. ☐
xviii. Wislows pay an hourly rate. ☐
 xix. Reg Vale is on extension 79. ☐
  xx. Harboys & Giddy want part-time workers. ☐

H Applying for a Job

Look at the advert below and then answer the following questions:

PRODUCTION OPERATORS

For Skilled Work on Day and Night Shifts on Trading Estate

Good basic rate plus overtime

All applications in writing with history of
previous employment to:
Mr. Wright,
H & D Weldings Ltd,
Main Road,
Industrial Estate

---

  i. How do you apply for the job? ....
 ii. What instructions are given? ....
iii. Who do you apply to? ....
 iv. What's the address? ....

I Comparing Methods of Application

Look at these three sections of advertisements.

*For further details
please contact*
Personnel Officer,
PESCOD LIMITED,
Eastern Avenue,
Industrial Estate.

Please write to–
J. Jones
Personnel Department
BULKO LIMITED.
Main Road,
Industrial Estate

Apply in Writing to:
Mrs. Owen.
JOHN & SONS LTD.,
High Street.

Write the answers to the questions in the table below:

	PESCOD LTD	BULKO LTD	JOHN & SONS LTD
How do you apply?			
Who do you apply to?			
What's the address?			

J How to Apply

Prospective employers may ask you to apply for a job in a particular way. Here are some examples:

1

APPLY IN PERSON

2

FOR FULL DETAILS RING:

3

WRITE WITH BRIEF DETAILS TO: Personnel Officer

4

PLEASE TELEPHONE OR CALL FOR FURTHER DETAILS

5

PLEASE RING 674021

6

TO ARRANGE INTERVIEW PLEASE CONTACT:

7

WRITE TO:

8

PLEASE WRITE FOR FURTHER DETAILS AND AN APPLICATION FORM TO:

9

FOR FURTHER INFORMATION WHY NOT CONTACT:

The main ways of applying for a job are *in writing, by phone* or *by calling in person/visiting*. List the above advertisements under these headings:

	In writing	By phone	Visiting
Example:		4	4

UNIT 6

FORMS AND JOB RECORDS

In Section A you will learn how to fill in a job application form. Section B looks at different people's work experience.

Section A
Focus:
Job Application Forms

Exercise 1: Filling in Forms

A Personal Details

Look at John Dolman's form and complete the form below with your own personal details.

SURNAME:	Dolman	Mr/~~Mrs/Miss/Ms~~
FIRST NAME(S):	John Paul	
ADDRESS:	44, Pinner Road	
	Boxend	
DATE OF BIRTH:	4 September 1956	
MARITAL STATUS:	Married	(married/single)

SURNAME:		Mr/Mrs/Miss/Ms
FIRST NAME(S):		
ADDRESS:		
DATE OF BIRTH:		
MARITAL STATUS:		(married/single)

B More of the same

Complete the form below with your own personal details:

FAMILY NAME	Mr/Mrs/Miss/Ms
CHRISTIAN NAME(S)	
PRESENT ADDRESS	
D.O.B.	
MARRIED	
SINGLE	
WIDOW	
WIDOWER	

C Looking at the differences

Compare the two forms on the opposite page and answer the questions:

i. What is another way of asking for your:

   a. family name? .... b. Christian name? ....

ii. What is another way of writing 'Date of birth'?

....

iii. What is another way of asking for your marital status?

....

D Describing Yourself

This is how John Dolman describes himself:

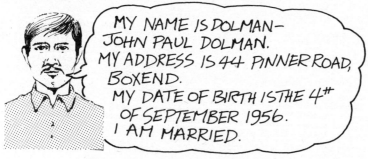

MY NAME IS DOLMAN— JOHN PAUL DOLMAN. MY ADDRESS IS 44 PINNER ROAD, BOXEND. MY DATE OF BIRTH IS THE 4th OF SEPTEMBER 1956. I AM MARRIED.

Now describe yourself, using the forms in Exercises A and B.

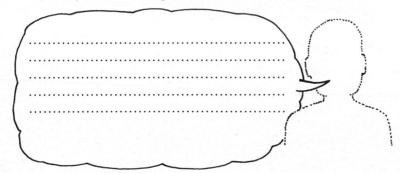

E Sorting Personal Details

Group the following words under the appropriate heading in the table.

Surname, Ms, Mr, christian name, permanent address, Mrs, family name, maiden name, Miss, forename, single, present address, widower, widow, male, second name, divorced, female, widowed, married.

NAME	ADDRESS	MARITAL STATUS	SEX

F School Details
Look at John Dolman's school details below.

DATES ATTENDED FROM:	TO:	SECONDARY SCHOOLS ATTENDED	EXAMINATIONS PASSED
4.9.67	14.7.71	Boxend Secondary School	'O' level: English, History, Geography, Mathematics, Biology, Chemistry, Physics.
7.9.71	2.7.73	Boxend Sixth Form College	'A' levels: Maths, Physics, Chemistry

Now complete the forms below with details of your education:

DATES ATTENDED FROM:	TO:	SECONDARY SCHOOLS ATTENDED	EXAMINATIONS PASSED

Name of school last attended ....

....

Dates attended ....
Exam successes ....

....

....

Name three subjects you have studied ....

....

What course are you on at the moment? ....

....

G School Report
This is how John Dolman talked about his school days:

I WENT TO BOXEND SECONDARY SCHOOL IN 1967.
FOUR YEARS LATER I TOOK 'O' LEVELS.
AFTER THAT I WENT TO THE SIXTH FORM COLLEGE AND I GOT 'A' LEVELS IN MATHEMATICS, PHYSICS AND CHEMISTRY IN 1973.

Now make a report on your school days, using the information on your form in Exercise F.

....

....

....

....

H Education Details
Read the following words and group them under the two headings in the table below:

School, examinations, secondary school, comprehensive school, institute, diploma, certificate, primary school, university, degree.

EDUCATIONAL ESTABLISHMENTS	QUALIFICATIONS

Exercise 2: Education and Qualifications

A Mavis Wall

This is Mavis Wall's further education record card:

FURTHER EDUCATION AND TRAINING	
COLLEGE	Mayford College of Further Education
DATES	September 1976 – July 1977
SUBJECTS	Typing Commercial Studies Shorthand English
QUALIFICATIONS	RSA Typing Pitman's Shorthand-Typing

Complete the following, using the information on Mavis Wall's record card:

When Mavis was sixteen she took CSE exams in English Literature, English Language, Science, Geography and History, and one 'O' level in Maths. With these qualifications she applied to .... of .... to do a course in .... and .... She was accepted and stayed at the college for .... year from .... to .... , taking the .... exam in typing and the .... exam in shorthand and typing in her final term.

B Abdul Aziz

Abdul Aziz went to school in England. Look at his forms below.
Listen to the tape and complete the general education form.

i. General Education

| SCHOOL | Primary: | | Comprehensive |
	Infant	Junior	
AGE			
SUBJECTS			
EXAMINATIONS			

ii. Further Education and Training
Now listen again and complete the Further Education and Training
Form.

COLLEGE	
DATES	
SUBJECTS	
QUALIFICATIONS GAINED	

C Your Form

i. Look at the forms below. Match the following words or letters with those on the form:

kind ....   year ....

month ....   studied ....

by letter ....   full time

write ....   study for

                                           one day only ....

ii. Fill in your own details on the two forms below.

GENERAL EDUCATION
Please give details of secondary schools attended:

Dates				Name of School	Type of School (Comprehensive, Independent, etc.)	Examinations (Give all subjects taken and results)
From		To				
m	y	m	y			

FURTHER EDUCATION AND TRAINING
Please give details of further education since leaving school, including training courses in industry. State (under 'Type of Training') if full-time, day release, evening or correspondence.

Dates				Name of University, College or other Institution	Type of Training	Subjects studied	Qualifications gained
From		To					
m	y	m	y				

UNIT 6

Section B
Focus: Job Records and Charts

Exercise 1: Records of Employment
A Bill Morris

Bill's Record

	DATES	JOB
WILSON'S LTD	1970–73	Packer
HUDSON'S	1973–75	Machine operator
E.P.I.	1975–	Capstan machine operator

Look at the table above giving details of Bill Morris's working career.
Answer the following questions.

    i. How many jobs has Bill Morris had? ....

   ii. When did he start work at Wilson's?   *in* ....

  iii. How long was he there?   *for* .... *from* .... *to* ....

  iv. What was his next job? ....

   v. Had he ever been a machine operator before? ....

  vi. Where is he working now? ....

 vii. What is his present job? ....

viii. How long has he had this job? ....

B Examining Bill's Record

This is how Bill Morris filled in his Employment History form:

EMPLOYMENT HISTORY

NAME & ADDRESS OF EMPLOYER	POSITION HELD	PERIOD: FROM TO	REASON FOR LEAVING
Wilson's Ltd, 281, Northumberland Avenue, Carlisle	Packer	1970–1973	Moved
J.B. Hudson & Co. Ltd, Wessex Way, Redmill Ind. Est., Mayford	Machine operator	1973–1975	Better prospects
E.P.I., 51 Greenhill Rd, Mayford	Capstan machine operator	1975 – present day	

Use the form to answer the following questions:

i. Why did he leave Wilson's?

....

ii. Where did he move to?

....

iii. What job did he get at Hudson's?

....

iv. Why did he move to E.P.I.?

....

v. Where is he now?

....

C Mark Ball

Mark's Record

	DATES	JOB	REASON FOR LEAVING
Wexfords, Churchill Way, Exford	1969–72	Labourer	Better wages: more money
E.M. Fraser Ltd, Caxton Street, Mayford	1972–75	Packer	Firm closed: redundant
W.M. Eldans, Smith Street, Mayford	1975–	Packer	

Using the above information, complete the following Employment History form for Mark Ball.

DATES From To	Name & Address of Employer	Job & Reason for Leaving

D Mrs Patel

1966–1970 worked at K & G Plastics as a packer. Left to have a baby. 1973–1976 worked at Bestons Biscuit Factory as a line operator. Moved to Southall, where she is living now.

Using this information, fill in the form on the next page for Mrs Patel's previous employment.

Mrs Patel's Record

Employer's Name	Nature of Business	Dates	Position held	Reason for leaving

E Bill Morris and his Job Record

Here is how Bill Morris talked about his job record.

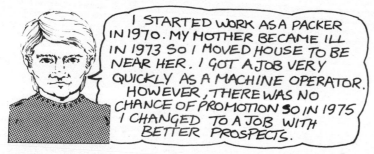

I STARTED WORK AS A PACKER IN 1970. MY MOTHER BECAME ILL IN 1973 SO I MOVED HOUSE TO BE NEAR HER. I GOT A JOB VERY QUICKLY AS A MACHINE OPERATOR. HOWEVER, THERE WAS NO CHANCE OF PROMOTION SO IN 1975 I CHANGED TO A JOB WITH BETTER PROSPECTS.

Look back at Exercises C and D and make a report on the employment records of Mark Ball and Mrs Patel.

MARK BALL

....

....

....

MRS PATEL

....

....

....

F Your Job Record

What about *your* employment history? Have you ever worked in this country before? If your answer is 'yes', list the last four jobs you have had, with dates, and then fill in the form below:

	JOB	DATES
i.	....	....
ii.	....	....
iii.	....	....
iv.	....	....

From	To	Name & Address of Employer	Nature of Duties	Salary on leaving	Reason for leaving

G

Now answer the following questions:

  i. How many jobs have you had in the last four years? ....

  ii. What was your last job? ....

  iii. Why did you leave? ....

  iv. What sort of job are you looking for now? ....

  v. Look back at Exercise E and make a report on *your* employment record.

....

....

....

....

....

....

Exercise 2: A Job Application Form

Complete this form with your details:

DATE.................... POSITION APPLIED FOR	

DATE................. POSITION APPLIED FOR ....

FIRST NAME(s) ....

SURNAME (BLOCK LETTERS PLEASE) ....

DATE OF BIRTH ....

ADDRESS (BLOCK LETTERS PLEASE) ....

....TELEPHONE NO. ....

HAVE YOU HAD ANY ILLNESS LIKELY TO AFFECT YOUR
EMPLOYMENT? .... YES/NO
IF YES Please give details ....

....

SCHOOL(S) ATTENDED SINCE AGE 11	DATES

EXAMINATIONS TAKEN/TO BE TAKEN:

SUBJECTS	LEVEL (CSE, GCE)	DATES	RESULTS (PLEASE GIVE GRADES)

(see over)

PLEASE GIVE BRIEF DETAILS OF HOBBIES AND SPORTS
ACTIVITIES
To include membership of any clubs, societies or sports teams

HAVE YOU ANY FRIENDS OR RELATIONS WHO WORK FOR US?
.... YES/NO
IF YES Please give name(s) and relationship

ON WHAT DAYS, IF ANY, ARE YOU *NOT* AVAILABLE FOR
INTERVIEW?

IS THERE ANY OTHER INFORMATION WHICH YOU THINK
WOULD BE OF INTEREST TO US?

SIGNED ....

UNIT 7

GETTING AN INTERVIEW

In this unit you will look at different ways of getting an interview. These include phoning about an advertisement and writing a letter of application. Finally you will look at the interview itself.

Section A
Focus: Letters and Telephone Calls

Exercise 1: Letter-writing

A

Select a job from Unit 3, and complete the letter below.

(*Your address*) ....

....

....

(*Today's date*) ....

Dear .... ,
I would like to apply for the job of .... I am
.... years old and have had a .... education.
I am .... and live in .... I would have no problems
getting to work. I could come for an interview ....

Yours ....

....

B Sorting out the Letter
Rearrange and write out the following in the space below to make a
letter applying for a job.

i.   23, High Road, Rochdale,
     Lancs.

ii. 5 December 1984

iii. Dear Sir, | I wish | for a
     job | as   a   canteen
     assistant | to apply

iv. in a canteen | I have already
     worked

v.   send me | please | an appli-
     cation form.

vi. faithfully | Yours

vii. Brown | Nora | (Miss)

....

....

....

....

....

....

....

....

C Addressing the envelope

Mr B. Frewing,
  Personnel Officer,
    Morning Forge Limited,
      26, Winton Road,
        MANCHESTER,
          MN6 2JY

Make sure you know:
 i. Where the stamp goes.
 ii. Where the address starts.
iii. What you write in capital letters.

Sort out the following addresses and write them down in the space below as if you were addressing an envelope:

i. Mr J. Robinson, | Smithers Ltd, | WA1 5MN | Personnel Manager, | WALSALL, | Staffs.

ii. Personnel Dept, | W.H. Lincoln & Co., | COVENTRY, | Wendover Way.

iii. Mrs Patterson, | Milford Industrial Estate, | Crawfords Ltd, | Birmingham.

....
....
....
....
....

D Finding an Address

Find out the addresses of these places in your town and write them down in the space below:

The Town Hall	Department of Health & Social
Hospital	Security
Inland Revenue	Job Centre or Employment
Industrial Health Clinic	Services Agency

....

....

....

....

....

....

....

....

E Points to Remember about Letter-writing

Read the text and then complete the following list:

When you write a letter use plain paper. Make sure that your letter is clear and neatly written, without any spelling mistakes or alterations. Read carefully the instructions that are given in the advertisement, and remember to answer any questions that are asked. Write your signature clearly at the end.

DO	DON'T
Use	Make ....
Write	Use ....
Follow	Forget ....
Answer	Make ....
Sign	

Exercise 2: Phoning About a Job

A Following the Instructions

> # MECHANICS
>
> ## for
>
> ## Clean Assembly Work
>
> with a young expanding organisation, which encourages effort with reward and has a genuine interest in every member of the staff.
>
> Usual holiday arrangements honoured.
>
> Knowledge of electrics and hydraulics advantageous.
>
> Immediate start for the right people.
>
> APPLY BY PHONE TO
> JOE BRYANT
> *SPEEDZ TRUCKS LTD*
> *Tel: 28800*
> *8, Turney Road*

Look at the advertisement above and answer the following questions:

i. What jobs are advertised? ....

ii. What's the name of the company? ....

iii. How do you apply? ....

iv. What's the phone number? ....

v. Who do you want to speak to? ....

vi. Why are you telephoning? ....

B Making the Call

Listen to the taped dialogue and then complete Mr Khan's part below:

Receptionist:	Smith's. Good morning.
Mr Khan:	Good morning. Can I speak to ....?
Receptionist:	Just a minute . . . you're through now.
Mr Khan:	Hello, ...?
Mr Jones:	Yes.
Mr Khan:	My name's .... I'm enquiring about the job advertised in ....
Mr Jones:	Oh, yes. Would you like to come for an interview?
Mr Khan:	Yes. When ....?
Mr Jones:	Could you come at 2 p.m. on Wednesday?
Mr Khan:	2 p.m. on .... Yes, yes I can.
Mr Jones:	Fine. Now when you come to the factory report to Reception and ask for me.
Mr Khan:	....
Mr Jones:	Right, see you Wednesday, Mr Khan. Good-bye.
Mr Khan:	Good-bye.

Now work with a partner and make up similar phone dialogues for B & N Products, Bell Engineering and Smith's.

COMPANY	PERSONNEL OFFICER	JOB	PLACE ADVERTISED
B & N PRODUCTS	Miss Robinson	Machine Operator	*The Advertiser*
BELL ENGINEERING	Mr Jenkins	Fitter	*The Express*
SMITH'S CHOCOLATE FACTORY	Mrs Roberts	Packer	*The Guardian*

C Enquiring About a Job

Listen to the taped dialogue and then complete Miss Jones's part below:

Receptionist:	Waltons. Good morning.
Miss Jones:	Can I speak to ....?
Receptionist:	Just a minute . . . you're through now.
Miss Jones:	....
Mr Smith:	Yes.
Miss Jones:	My name's .... I'm interested in .... you have advertised in ....
Mr Smith:	Well, it's Grade 4 permanent day work. .... Are you still interested?
Miss Jones:	Oh yes.
Mr Smith:	Would you like to come for an interview?
Miss Jones:	Yes. I ....
Mr Smith:	That would be fine. Would 11 a.m. be all right?
Miss Jones:	Yes, ...
Mr Smith:	O.K. See you tomorrow then, Miss Jones. Good-bye.
Miss Jones:	Good-bye.

Now work with a partner and phone Bulko Ltd, A.E.F. & Co. Ltd. and Waltons.

COMPANY	PERSONNEL OFFICER	JOB	JOB DETAILS
BULKO LTD.	Mrs Finn	Labourer	Shift work
A.E.F. & CO.LTD.	Mr May	Storeman	Day work
WALTONS BISCUITS	Mrs Craven	Canteen assistant	Part-time

D Vacancy Filled
Listen to the taped dialogue and then complete Mr Singh's part below:

Receptionist: Good morning.

Mr Singh: Good morning. Can I speak to ....
....?

Receptionist: Just a minute . . . the line is engaged. Will you hold?

Mr Singh: Yes, ...

Receptionist: I'm putting you through now.

Mr Singh: Hello, ...

Mr Oliver: Yes. Can I help you?

Mr Singh: I saw your advertisement for a ....

....

last week, I . . .

Mr Oliver: I'm sorry. The vacancy has been filled. The new employee started on Monday.

Mr Singh: Oh, I see. Do you have ....

Mr Oliver: Sorry, no.

Mr Singh: O.K. then. Sorry for ....

Mr Oliver: That's all right. Good-bye.

Mr Singh: Good-bye.

Now work with a partner and phone B & N Products, Bell Engineering and A.E.F.

COMPANY	APPLICANT	PERSONNEL OFFICER	JOB
B & N PRODUCTS	Mr King	Mrs Robinson	Packer
BELL ENGINEERING	Miss Roy	Mr Jenkins	Secretary
A.E.F. & CO.LTD.	Mr Brook	Mr May	Gateman

E Making an Appointment for an Interview
Listen to the taped dialogue and then complete Mrs Armstrong's part below:

Receptionist:	Boltons. Good morning.
Mrs Armstrong:	Good morning. Can I have ....?
Receptionist:	Just a minute . . . the line is engaged. Will you hold?
Mrs Armstrong:	Yes, please.
Receptionist:	I'm putting you through now.
Mrs Armstrong:	Hello. My name's .... I saw your advertisement for .... Are there still vacancies?
Personnel Officer:	Yes. Can you let me have your name and address and I'll make an appointment for an interview for you.
Mrs Armstrong:	The name is .... and my address is ....
Personnel Officer:	Paula Armstrong, 14 Falmouth Road. Right, now, can you come on Tuesday, at 10.00 a.m.?
Mrs Armstrong:	.... Yes, yes, I can.
Personnel Officer:	When you come to the factory, report to Reception and say that you have come for an interview.
Mrs Armstrong:	O.K. ....
Personnel Officer:	That's all right. Good-bye for now.
Mrs Armstrong:	Good-bye.

Now work with a partner and phone Bulko Ltd, Waltons Biscuits and B & N Products.

COMPANY	CALLER	ADDRESS
BULKO LTD	Mary Merton	1, Church Way
WALTONS BISCUITS	John Cory	13, Leafy Drive
B & N PRODUCTS	Bill Simms	29, Ashbourne Road

F Getting Job Details

Listen to the taped dialogue and then complete Mr Morgan's part below:

Receptionist:	G.B.K. Good morning.
Mr Morgan:	Good morning. Can I have ....?
Receptionist:	Hold the line, please . . . you're through now.
Mr Smith:	Hello, Mr Smith speaking.
Mr Morgan:	Hello. My name is .... I'm interested in .... advertised in today's .... Could you send me the details please?
Mr Smith:	Yes, certainly. Let me take your name and address. What did you say your name was?
Mr Morgan:	....
Mr Smith:	How do you spell that?
Mr Morgan:	....
Mr Smith:	And your initials?
Mr Morgan:	....
Mr Smith:	Now your address please?
Mr Morgan:	....
Mr Smith:	15 Liverpool Road. O.K. I'll get those details off to you right away.
Mr Morgan:	Thank you very much.
Mr Smith:	That's all right. Good-bye.
Mr Morgan:	....

Now work with a partner and phone Boltons Ltd, John and Sons Ltd and Hargreaves Ltd.

COMPANY	CALLER'S NAME AND ADDRESS	
BOLTONS LTD	Dave King	15, Monmouth Street
JOHN & SONS LTD	Mary White	50, Merton Avenue
HARGREAVES LTD	Anna Sutton	23, Oxford Road

TRESCOLDS LIMITED

We urgently require

PACKERS

for our Production
Department

Starting salary £56 per week
Monday to Friday 8.00 a.m. – 5.00 p.m.
Generous Holidays and Pension Scheme

Apply by phone to:

Mr Sealey,
Personnel Department
Tel: 34527

With a partner, complete the following telephone conversation, using information from the above advertisement.
Then complete the conversation in writing below:

Receptionist:	Trescolds .... Can I help you?
Applicant:	....
Receptionist:	Yes. Who's calling?
Applicant:	....
Receptionist:	Just a moment.
Personnel:	Good morning.
Applicant:	....
Personnel:	Yes.
Applicant:	....
Personnel:	Have you worked as a packer before?
Applicant:	....
Personnel:	How long were you there?
Applicant:	....
Personnel:	Why did you leave, then?
Applicant:	....
Personnel:	I see. Can you come and see me tomorrow afternoon?
Applicant:	....
Personnel:	About 2.30 p.m.
Applicant:	....
Personnel:	Thank you. Good-bye.
Applicant:	....

H Points to Remember about Phoning
Read the text and then complete the following list.

When you phone about a job make sure you have the advertisement in front of you. Speak slowly and clearly and ask for the right person. Give your own name and be ready to answer questions about your experience and qualifications. Be ready to tell the company when you can go for an interview. Remember to write down any information you are given.

DO	DON'T
have	leave ....
ask for	forget ....
speak	answer ....
give	forget ....
answer	
be ready	
have	

88

UNIT 7

Section B
Focus:
The Interview

Exercise 1: At the Job Centre

A The Job Centre Interview

JOBCENTRE

(MAN OR WOMAN)

JOB	– Canteen assistant Age 16 +
DISTRICT	– Town centre
BUSINESS	–
PAY	– £56 per week at age 18+
HOURS	– 8.30 – 5.45 Mon – Thurs; 6.15 Friday
DETAILS	– Various duties, including serving at counter, clearing tables, collecting trays, etc. May help with food preparation. Exp. preferred. High standard of hygiene essential.

ASK FOR JOB No. 2325

Look at the card and listen to the dialogue. Then, working with a partner, complete similar interviews for the other job cards.
Use the following outline to help you:

You: ....

Interviewer: Good morning. Can I help you?

You: ....

Interviewer: The ....job?

You: ....

Interviewer: Have you ever worked before?

You: ....

Interviewer: Well, I'll phone the company and see if the situation is still vacant. What's your name?

You: ....

Interviewer: How old are you?

You: ....

Interviewer: When would you be free to visit the company?

You: ....

Interviewer: If you'd like to take a seat I'll ring the company.

i.

JOBCENTRE

(MAN OR WOMAN)

JOB	Capstan setter operator
DISTRICT	Slough
BUSINESS	—
PAY	Neg.
HOURS	8.00 – 4.45 Monday – Friday
DETAILS	Set and operate capstan to machine piece parts using stainless steel. Also set and operate centre lathe. Must be fully skilled and exp., preferably with exp. of copy turning.

ASK FOR JOB No. 2849

ii.

JOBCENTRE

(MAN OR WOMAN)

JOB	Spray painter
DISTRICT	Coventry
BUSINESS	—
PAY	Negotiable
HOURS	8.00 – 5.00 Monday – Friday
DETAILS	Work on car accident repairs. Rub down surfaces, mix paint to required colour, and spray. Must be skilled.

ASK FOR JOB No. 6643

iii

JOBCENTRE

(MAN OR WOMAN)

JOB	Post room worker
DISTRICT	Oxford
BUSINESS	Publisher
PAY	Under review
HOURS	8.00 – 5.00 Monday – Friday
DETAILS	Sort and deliver post; collect and distribute internal mail; prepare packages and letters for dispatch; relief switchboard operator. No exp. nec.

ASK FOR JOB No. 4411

Exercise 2: At the Factory

A Going for Interview — Five Tips
Find the words in column C that go with the words in column A.
Write them in the correct order in column B.

A	B	C
Be sure you Allow yourself Find out Look Think about		enough time to get there smart know the time and place questions to ask about the firm and job.

B Points to Remember at the Interview
Read the following and put them under the correct heading in the chart:

be nervous	listen to questions
be polite	answer questions
be friendly	worry
look at the interviewer	look interested
ask questions	criticise past employers
smoke	

DO	DON'T

C Applying for a Job at a Factory

Look at the two vacancy boards below and listen to the taped conversations that go with them.

i.

VACANCIES

ii.

VACANCIES
PACKERS Apply within

With a partner, make up similar conversations in which you enquire about a factory job.

Use the information on the three vacancy boards below:

iii.

VACANCIES
Assembly work available Apply at Reception

iv.

VACANCIES
....

v.

VACANCIES
Machine operator Apply within

D Interview Strategies

Look at the chart below and listen to the conversation on the tape between Mrs Giles and the Personnel Officer. Does Mrs Giles do well at her interview? Complete the chart below with a few words on how well you think she did.

Explaining unemployment:
Reassuring the employer:
Anything else?

Using information from the chart below, practise similar job interviews with a partner.

	MRS DODD	MR BROOKS	MS ROBINS
Explaining unemployment:	Young children	Made redundant	Recently left college
Reassuring the employer:	Mother lives next door	Wife can look after the children	Not married, no children
Anything else?	No. 11 bus goes past the house	Lives on a bus route	Own transport

E More strategies

Look at the table below. Listen to Mr Benson's interview on the tape and complete the table.

What does Mr Benson say about . . .
i. His present job? ....
ii. His reason for leaving it? ....
iii. His journey to the new job? ....
iv. Overtime? ....

Using information from the chart below, practise similar job interviews with a partner.

	MR MURPHY	MRS HILL	MS HUGHES
Present job:	Clerk	Cook	Training officer
Reason for leaving	Better pay	Bigger kitchen, more variety	More responsibility
Journey to new job:	Regular service by train	Only five minutes away	Car
Overtime:	Saturday mornings only	No	————